The Robot

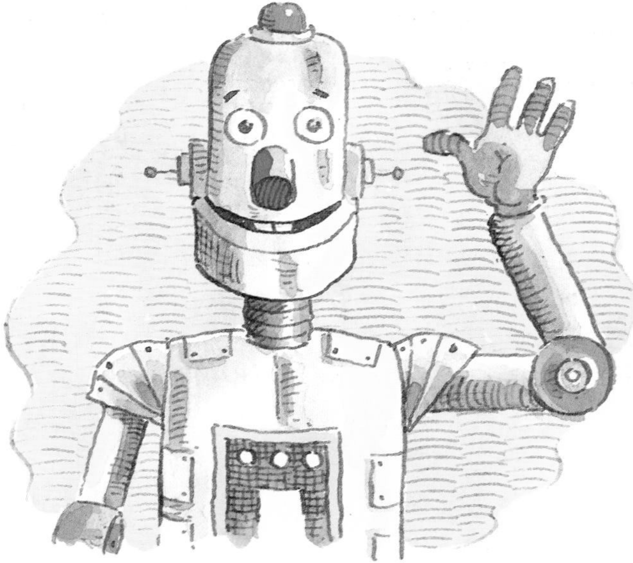

Story by Tony Mitton
Illustrations by Phil Garner

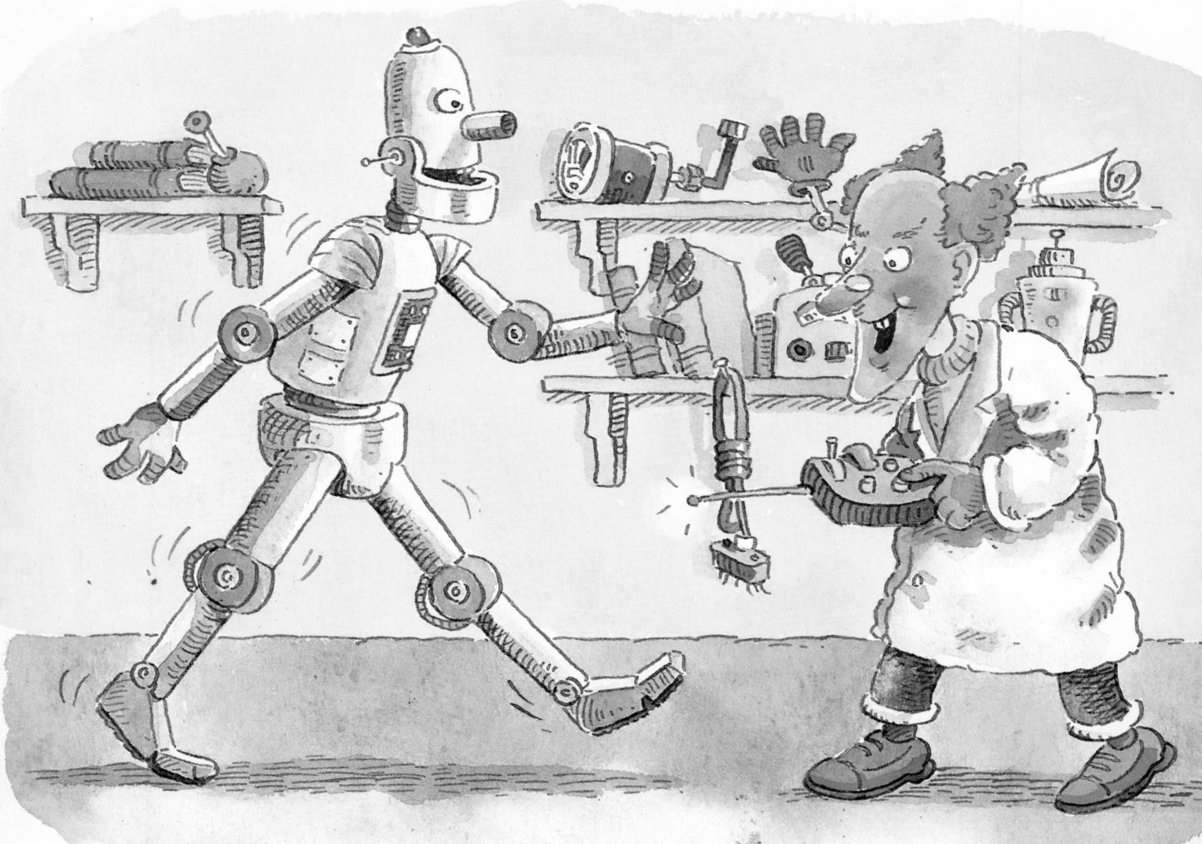

It can walk!

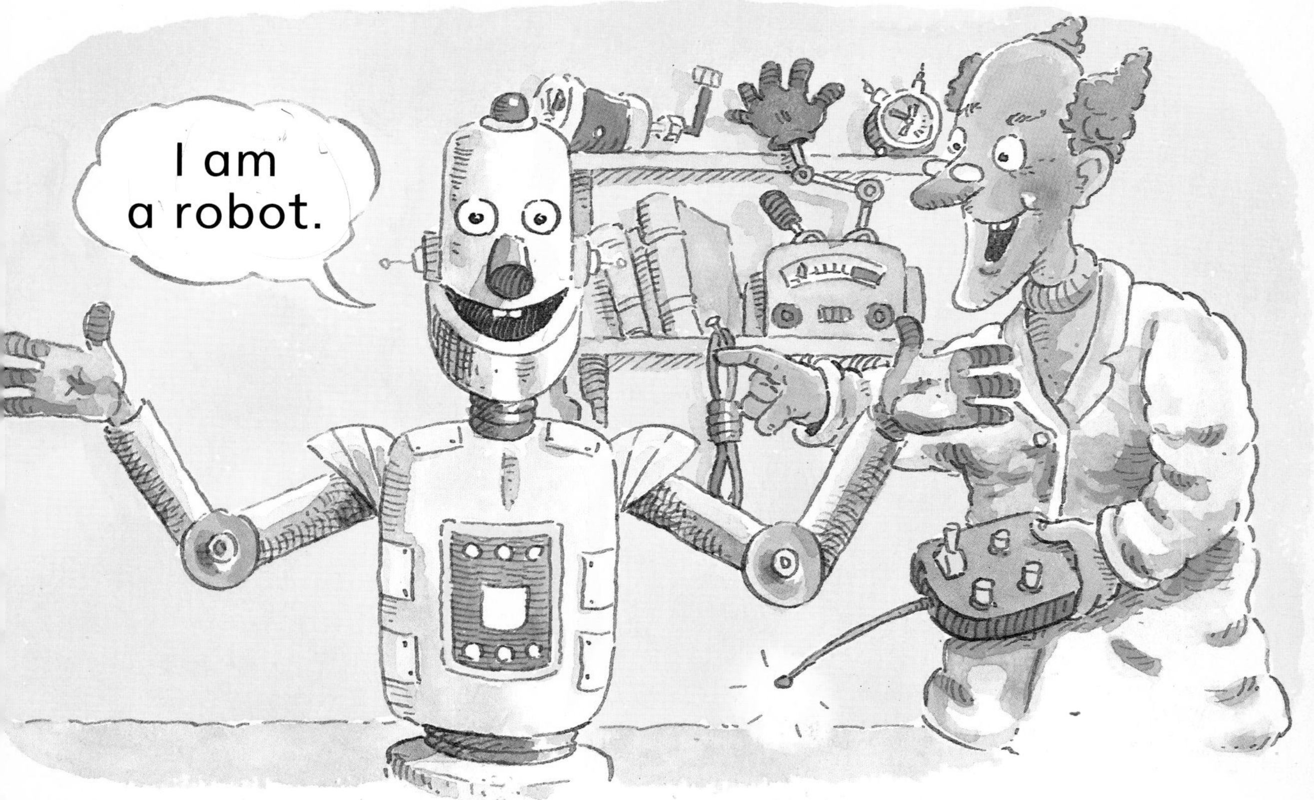

It can talk!

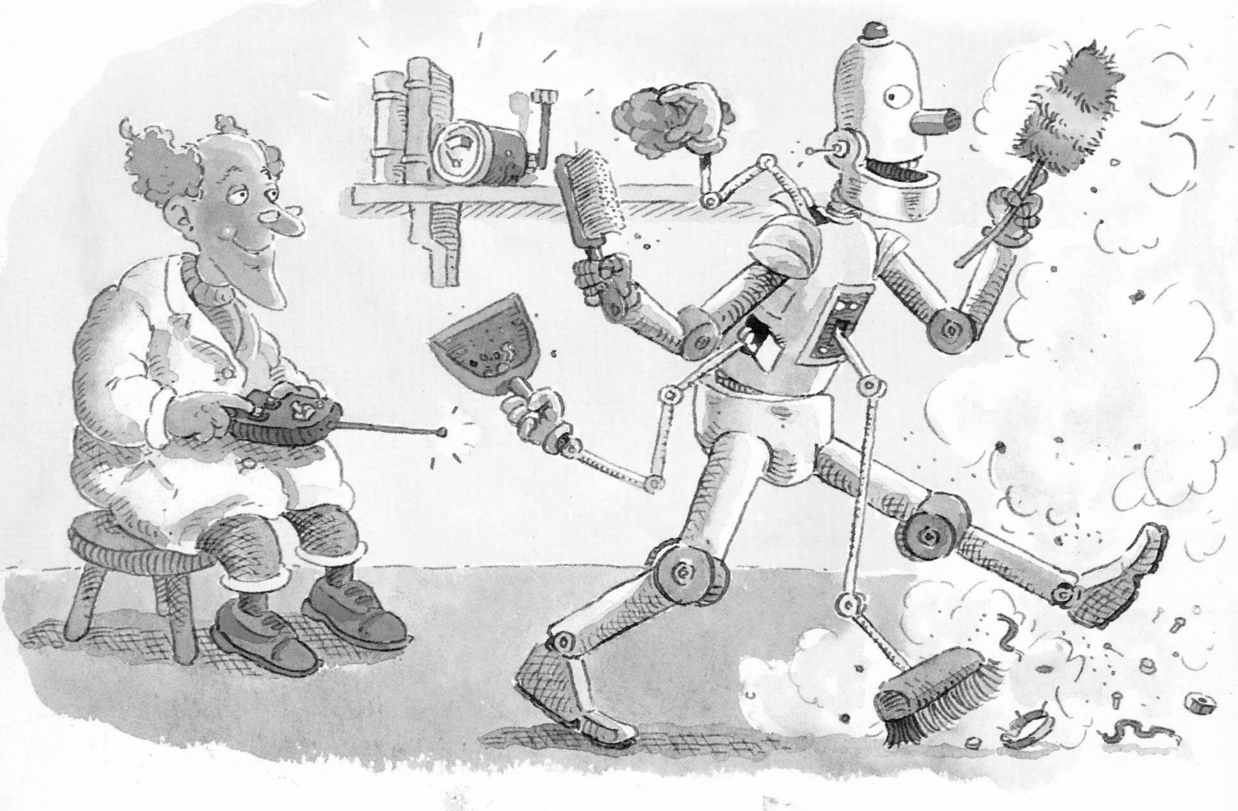

It can clean!

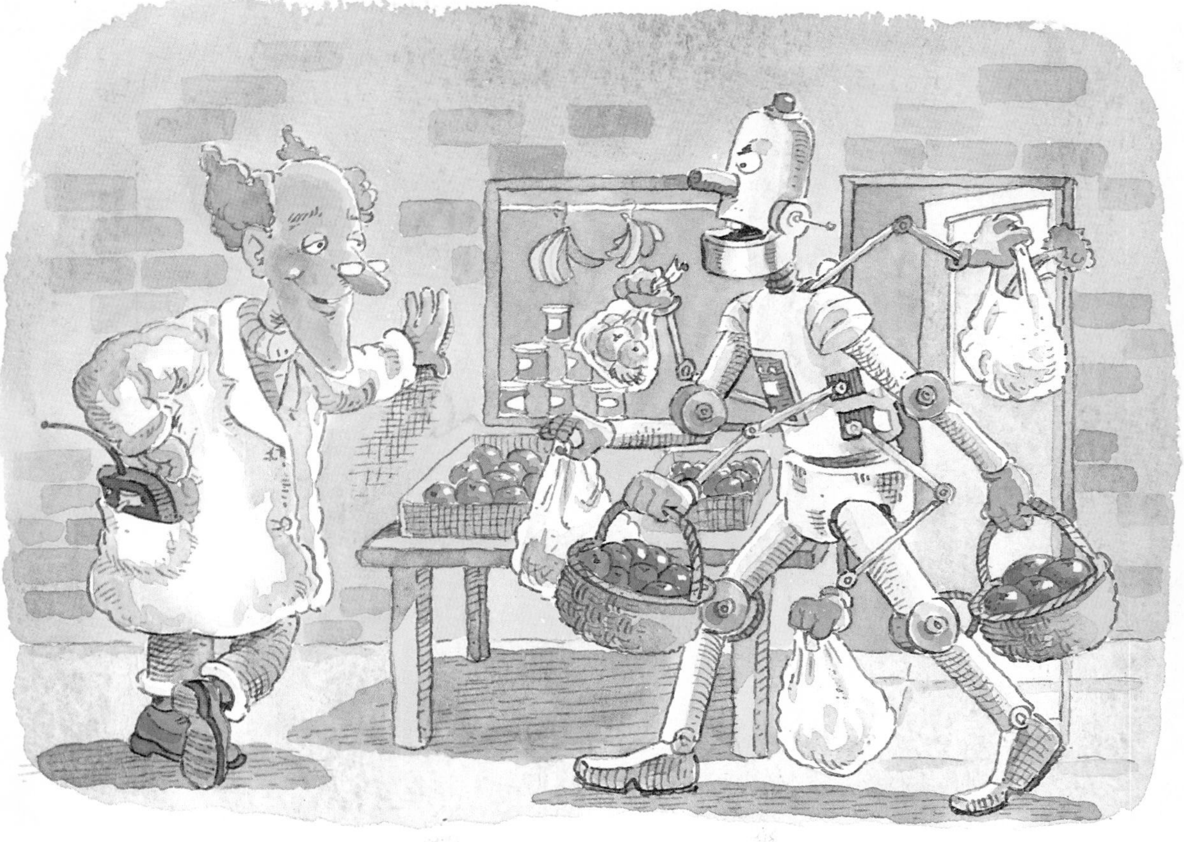

It can shop!

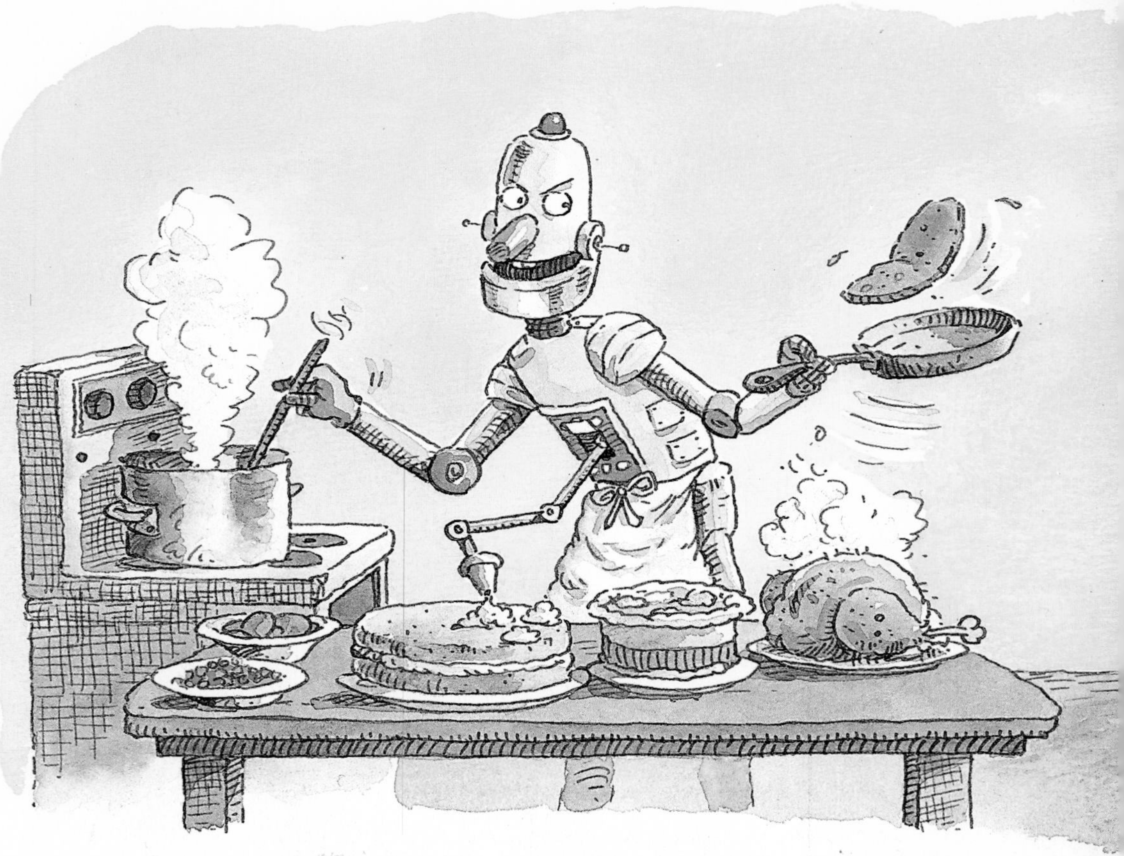

It can cook!

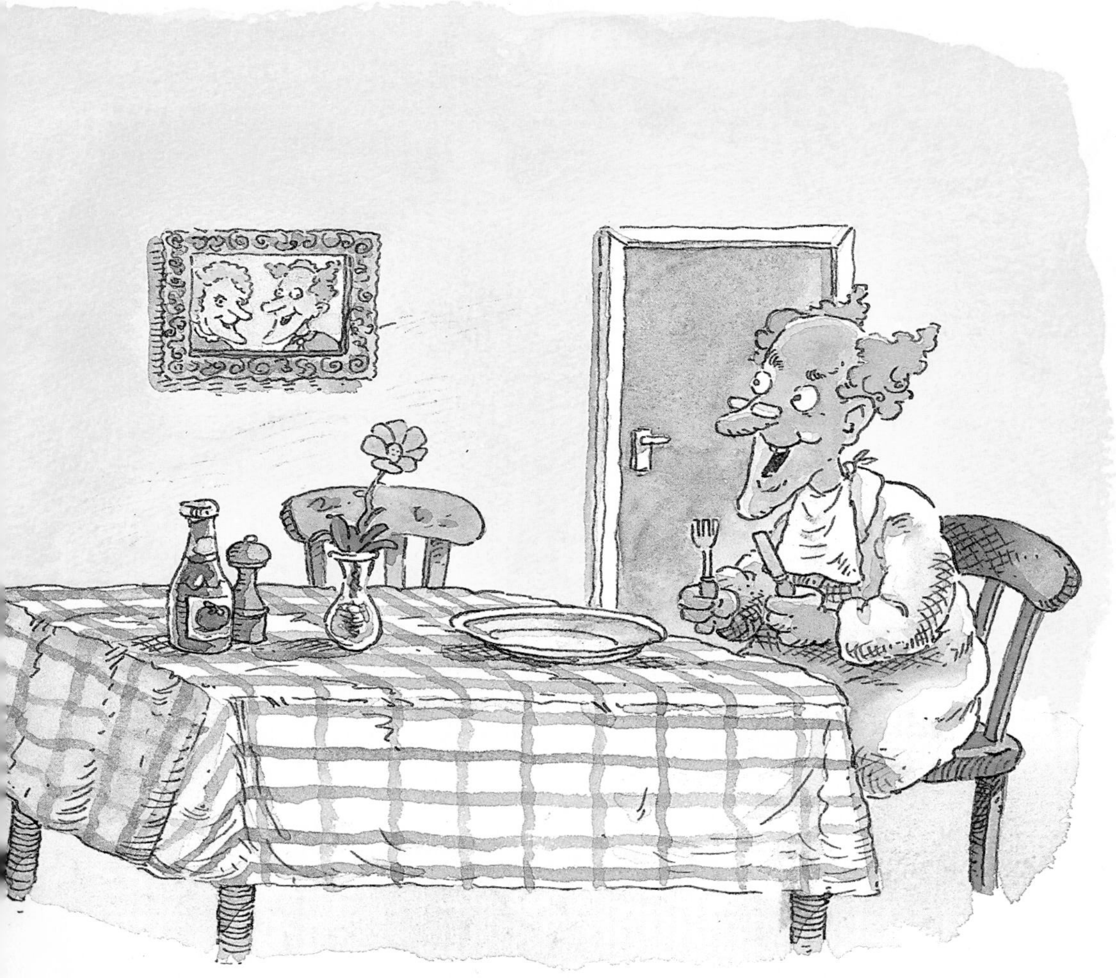

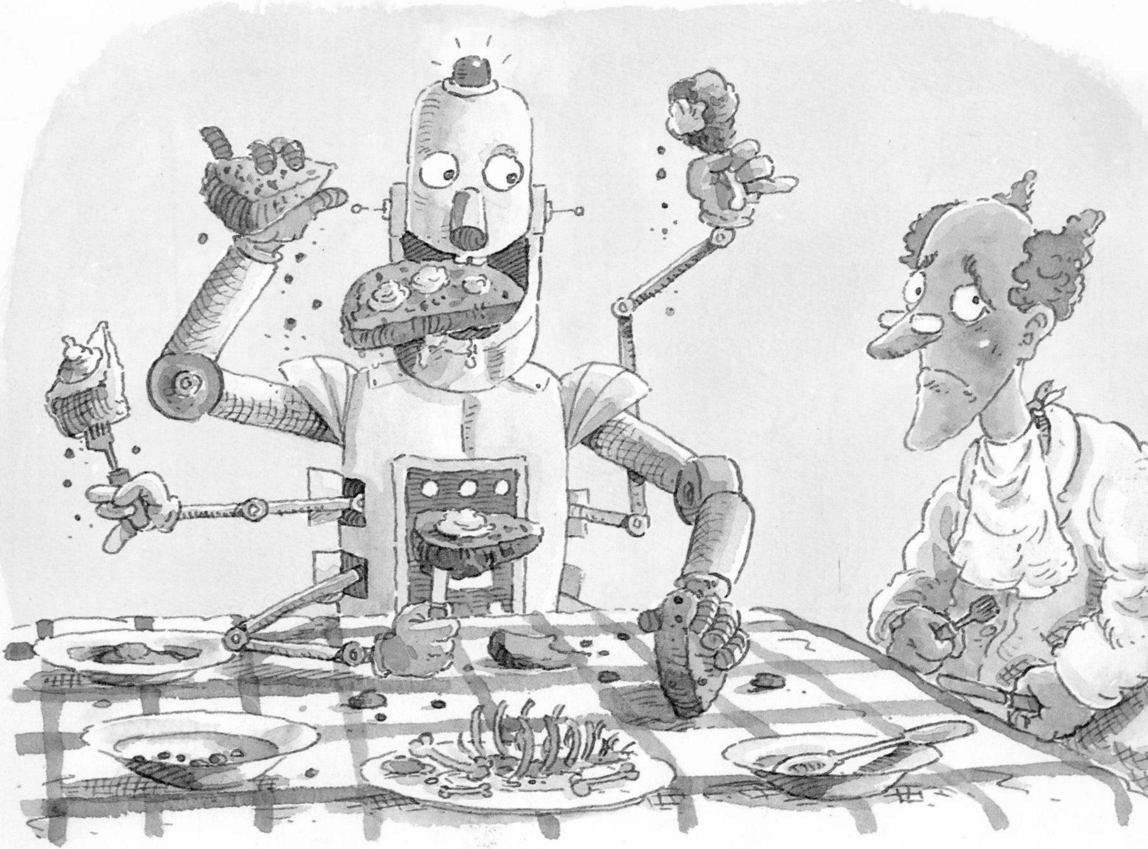

It can eat!